What Does Sunlight Do?

by Jennifer Boothroyd

first step nonfiction

Lerner Publications Company · Minneapolis

Copyright © 2015 by Lerner Publishing Group, Inc.

All rights reserved. International copyright secured. No part of this book may be reproduced, stored in a retrieval system, or transmitted in any form or by any means—electronic, mechanical, photocopying, recording, or otherwise—without the prior written permission of Lerner Publishing Group, Inc., except for the inclusion of brief quotations in an acknowledged review.

The images in this book are used with the permission of: © Johnny-ka/Shutterstock.com, p. 4; © Roman Sakhno/Shutterstock.com, p. 5; © iStock/Thinkstock, p. 6; © iStockphoto.com/EHStock, p. 7; © iStockphoto.com/titlezpix, p. 8; © oriontrail/Shutterstock.com, p. 9; © Vaclav Volrab/Shutterstock.com, p. 10; © Suppakij1017/Shutterstock.com, p. 11; © iStockphoto.com/GlobalStock, p. 12; © mycola/Shutterstock.com, p. 13; © iStockphoto.com/ivafet, p. 14; © iStockphoto.com/Christopher Bernard, p. 15; © Purestock/Thinkstock, p. 16; © iStockphoto.com/digitalskillet, p. 17; © iStockphoto.com/Vandervelden, p. 18; © Ivonne Wierink/Shutterstock.com, p. 19; © Creatas/Thinkstock, p. 20; © istock/Thinkstock, p. 21; © iStockphoto.com/OceanFishing, p. 22.

Front Cover: iStockphoto/zmeel.

Main body text set in ITC Avant Garde Gothic Std Medium 21/25.
Typeface provided by Adobe Systems.

Lerner Publications Company
A division of Lerner Publishing Group, Inc.
241 First Avenue North
Minneapolis, MN 55401 USA

For reading levels and more information, look up this title at www.lernerbooks.com.

Library of Congress Cataloging-in-Publication Data

Cataloging-in-Publication Data for *What Does Sunlight Do?* is on file at the Library of Congress.
ISBN: 978–1–4677–3921–4 (LB)
ISBN: 978–1–4677–4679–3 (EB)

Manufactured in the United States of America
1 – CG – 7/15/14

Table of Contents

Sunlight

The sun is a star.

Sunlight comes from the **sun**.

We need light to see. The
sun gives us light.

Sunlight brightens the sky.

The sun even makes light
on cloudy days.

The sun peeks through these trees.

The sun rises early in the morning.

Sunlight is strong
in early afternoon.

The sun climbs higher later
in the day.

9

The sun has started to set.

The sun sets in the evening.

The moon gives a little light.
It reflects the sun's light.

By nighttime, it is dark.

Sunlight gives us heat.

This ground is hot and dry.

It heats the ground.

This lizard gets heat from the sun.

Sunlight warms the animals.

14

It heats water.

Sunlight is stronger in **summer**.

There is less sunlight in
winter.

Using Sunlight

Clothes dry in the sunlight.

Sunlight has many uses.

Plants need sunlight to grow.

Vitamin D makes
our bones strong.

Our bodies need sunlight to
make vitamin D.

These panels catch sunlight.

We make sunlight into **electricity**.

Why do you like sunlight?

Glossary

electricity – a type of energy

summer – a season between spring and fall

sun – the star in the center of Earth's orbit

winter – a season between fall and spring

Index